MY BOOK OF SILLY

POEMS

AND THINGS

Angela Ryles

ISBN: 978-1503254510
         1503254518

Copyright belongs to the author

British Library Cataloguing in Publication data.

All rights reserved. No part of this anthology may be reproduced in any form or by any means—graphic, electronic or mechanical means, including but not limited to printing, file sharing and email, without prior consent from the author.

Apart from my memoirs and reminiscences, names, characters and incidents in this book are products of the author's imagination or are used fictionally.

Cover design by Annette Jones
Published by Angela Rigley
www.nunkynoo.yolasite.com

Copyright © 2014, Angela Rigley

INTRODUCTION

Hi, welcome to this, my first anthology of poems and short stories, most of them silly, but all of them as daft as me. There are also some of the Thoughts for the Day that I write and broadcast for Radio Nottingham.

I dedicate this book to my five children and eight grandchildren, and also to The Eastwood Writers' Group, whose help and encouragement have made this book possible.

My other books, published by www.bluewoodpublishing are also available on Amazon:
   Looking for Jamie,
   A Dilemma for Jamie
   School for Jamie

My websites are:
   www.nunkynoo.yolasite.com
   www.authoryantics.wordpress.com
   Find me on Facebook, LinkedIn, Goodreads, and Twitter: www.twitter.com/angierigley

CONTENTS

Clarice the Chair	7
Memoirs Chapter 1	9
Are we Nearly There	15
Recycling (Thought for the Day)	17
Autumn Leaves	18
On Heron's Wings	19
The Clock	27
Autumnal Morn	30
Lambs (Thought)	32
Tooth Be or not Tooth Be	33
A Limerick	38
Highwayhorse	39
Me Drop to Sleep	41
Nightmare	44
Bluetit's Revenge	47
Sparrows (Thought)	49

The Presentation	50
Free-falling	52
Not Working	53
Coincidences (Thought)	55
Ode to my Mother	57
Six Geese a-laying	58
Competition Page	60
Interlopers (Thought)	62
Moo	63
Peter's New Bike	65
Nightmare Part 2	66
Fading Eyesight	68
Birdsong (Thought)	69
Roses	70
Memoirs Chapter 2: Pets	72
Nature	78
Angel Voices	79
Gentleman on the Bus	81

Like a Bird	83
My Family Tree	85
A Day in the Woods	87
Easter Sunday Spectacle	89
The Ring	90
My Garden	92
Homesick	94
Scardey Cat	95
Forgotten Present	97
Nightmare Part 3	99
Final Thought	101

CLARICE THE CHAIR ON HOLIDAY

'Now where shall I sit?'
mumbles Clarice the Chair.
'In front of this wall
or perhaps over there?
I liked where I sat
yesterday on the lawn,
so I stayed there all night
'til the onset of dawn.
But I think I'd prefer
to move nearer the flowers,
and sniff the red roses
for a while, maybe hours.
Or shall I divert
to a place by the stream,
where the birdsong will send me
to sleep and to dream?
I must make up my mind,
for I still haven't found
the best spot to park.
I want somewhere that's sound,
perhaps near to the shrubs
where I can keep out of sight,
and no-one will find me
'til later tonight.

I won't have fat bottoms
slouching onto my seat,
or tea spills or coffee
or foul, cheesy feet.
Yes, I think I'll do that,
I'll hide under the trees,
and sway to the swell
of a soft, gentle breeze.
Ah! This is the life.
What a fine peaceful spot.
Oh, no! That bird's plopped on me.
Well, thanks a lot.

MEMOIRS

The First Chapter

I came into the world at five o'clock on Friday the ninth of May 1947, in a farm cottage in Piddinghoe, just outside Peacehaven, in Sussex. During my childhood, actually all my life, I preferred to tell everybody I was born in Peacehaven. It sounds so much more, well peaceful, I suppose, and in keeping with my name, doesn't it?

My mother used to tell me I was born just as my father was getting up for work. I have visions of him sleeping peacefully whilst my mother and the midwife laboured quietly beside him, not wanting to disturb him, because he had a hard day ahead of him on the farm, and him waking up saying, "Oh, another one? Well done, see you later," as he went out the door. Well, I was the fifth child to survive. Apparently my mother had fourteen pregnancies, but only eight of us lived.

Some years ago, whilst on holiday for our annual filial get-together in Brighton, two of my older sisters and I decided to see if the farm cottages were still there—we moved to

Hampshire when I was six months old—but it was a wet, blustery day and when we eventually found the lane, it said '2 miles to Piddinghoe', so we enquired about a bus. One did run there but only once a week! Needless to say, we didn't go, but we looked around Peacehaven and found the cottage that my family had lived in before my parents moved to the farm. That looked very much as my sisters remembered it.

Then, in 2014, on another reunion, we visited Falmer, just outside Brighton, where our grandparents lived until their deaths in the 1950s. Their grave is there, in which our father, his oldest brother and his oldest sister, who died tragically from an infected bite, are also buried.

On previous visits there had never been anyone in at the cottage but, this year, the lady was washing the caravan on the drive so, Mike, my brother, spoke to her. Lo and behold, she had known our grandparents, and had actually lived a few doors away as a child. She remembered Granny as a tall, elegant woman. I only recall seeing her once, when I was about nine, sitting in the doorway of the cottage—a little old lady with white hair.

We moved to Hill Farm near Lasham, Basingstoke when I was six months old, and lived there until I was five, soon after I had started at St Joseph's Catholic school in Basingstoke. This involved walking nearly a mile to the main road, catching a bus into town with my sister, Barbi, who is four years older than me, and then a short walk to school, and of course, doing the opposite on the way home. I don't think I was a puny child, but the travelling became too much for me, so I started at the local infant school which still needed the mile walk, but the bus journey was shorter. I wasn't there long as we moved soon afterwards to a different farm, a few miles the other side of Basingstoke, where we lived for four years.

Again we were sent to the local village school, this time in Ramsdell, because there was not a regular bus, even though we were on a main road. The farmer who owned the farm paid for us to go there in a taxi. Wow, I'd never been in a taxi before. I don't remember much about this school, except having to go out of the classroom and sit in the hallway while the other children had religious lessons, as, being a

Roman Catholic, I was not allowed to participate. How times have changed!

When we first moved there we lived in a tiny cottage where, once a week, we took turns in a tin bath in front of the fire, all in the same water, with the oldest going first and the younger ones all jumping in together. After a while we moved across the road to a brand new house, with a bathroom. We weren't supposed to go near the site when they were building, of course, but I couldn't resist going as close as possible and sniffing the new wood being used on the roofs. Whenever I smell new wood I close my eyes and savour that fragrance, and remember how much I loved it.

I look back on those four years as the happiest of my childhood, probably because there were more children to play with than at any other time. It was a small close-knit community. One of the neighbour's sons had callipers on his legs but he could run as fast, if not faster, than the rest of us. We would play a game of sitting by the roadside, swallowing little, round pebbles and bringing them back up. My sister, Gina, couldn't do it and still bemoans her lack of skill to Mike and me. Goodness knows how her stomach must have suffered.

When I was ten, we moved to yet another farm in between Basingstoke and Alton, at Burkham, again about a mile from the main road and transport. The bus didn't run on Sundays so we went to church in Basingstoke on a Saturday morning. The nuns in the convent next door to the church used to invite us for a cup of tea and biscuits after Mass. Somehow that tea had a special smell and, very occasionally, I catch a whiff of it nowadays, and my mind goes back to those visits.

One Saturday, I was skipping along on the way home, jumping on everyone's shadows, when I tripped and badly gashed my leg. I hobbled home and Daddy was very concerned. Well, as my siblings tell me—I don't think enviously—I was his favourite. He dug out the Savlon antiseptic cream and squeezed the tube, squirting the cream, not onto my leg, but all down the door. Everyone burst out laughing, even me. I seem to remember I was a good little girl, a 'lily-white hen' as Mummy called me, but I disobeyed her order not to play on the stilts at school while I still had the scab. You can guess what happened. But I had never fallen off them before!

That house had no running water. My mother had to fetch it in buckets from across the road, and it played havoc with her internal workings. She was rushed into hospital. Barbi, being a senior, had been attending the Convent at Alton, while the rest of us went to St Joseph's again in Basingstoke. Mummy wrote a letter to the Reverend Mother to ask if Barbi, myself and Gina could be boarders. We were accepted and packed off the next day.

I had missed the eleven plus exam, because I had changed schools just at the time of registration, but it did not matter, somehow. The Convent was a private grammar school and we could not afford the fees, so were kept on as charity cases. It was a struggle for Mummy just to buy our uniforms.

We moved house soon afterwards, on the advice of the doctors, to West Clandon, near Guildford. One time, walking home from the railway station for the school holidays, I prayed all the way that my parents would not have moved and forgotten to tell me. I was about eleven by then.

ARE WE NEARLY THERE YET?

Are we nearly there yet?
a voice comes from behind.

"Not quite, my dear,
wind your window down,
and look at those baby lambs,
frolicking and gambolling
in the field;
the big ones with horns are the rams.
See that colourful pheasant,
its plumage so bright
and there on the lake is a swan.
You usually love to look at the birds.
Don't tell me, my dear,
that I'm wrong.

But aren't we nearly there yet?
I'm getting bored, you know.

Just look at the bluebells
spread right through the woods,
clumps of primroses, cowslips there too,
lots of bushes of broom
and sharp, prickly gorse,

hosts of daffodils, yellow in hue.
A waterfall's tumbling down the hill,
droplets sending up vibrant rainbows;
and moss, covering walls and
chopped-off tree stumps,
looks like blotches
of green marshmallows.

*Please say we're nearly there, Mum.
How much further is it?*

We've come to the Lakes,
to get our walking boots on;
to be free, to relax and to rest,
away from the hustle and bustle of life,
so please, darling,
stop being a pest.
No, of course, there isn't
a penny arcade,
we are here with ne'er a care;
so stop asking about sea,
and donkeys and sand.
Just breathe in the mountain air.

*But, Mum surely we can't really be there?
Oh, it's not fair.*

RECYCLING (A Thought for the Day)

I recycle as much as I can, obsessively so, in my family's opinion, so useful materials can be reused, instead of being sent to the communal tip or burned. As I sit in the garden or in the park, listening to the birds singing, trying to identify the different tunes, I often thank God for giving me such appreciation. The beauty of an autumn day, with the orange and amber colours of the trees around me, fills me with delight, as does the sight of the first primrose opening its petals to the watery spring sun. Summer days spent at the seaside with the family live on in my memory, and the sight of snow falling when I am tucked up in my warm and cosy lounge can't stifle my thankfulness for all God's wonders. I pray that our world will stay as wonderful, and not turn to ruin, once the bees and pollinating insects are all eradicated by pollutants and pesticides, or the effects of so-called global warming take hold, and flooding becomes a daily occurrence. I'd better put out my bin and plant some more bee-friendly flowers quickly, before it's too late.

AUTUMN LEAVES

In the sighing sough
of an autumn breeze,
or the biting bursts
of a gusting gale,
tall trees, almost bare,
shed useless leaves,
their purpose o'er,
now green no more;
they twizzle and twirl
in a demon dance;
amber, orange, brown and gold,
gyrating in circles in the dust;
swirling, spinning,
they seem still alive,
driven by some unseen force.
Crunchy piles tempt little boots
to jump inside,
or scrunch underfoot.
The glade resounds with kicks of glee,
echoed by birds
in the now bare trees.

ON HERON'S WINGS

I wander down towards the river. Need to get away. Jack and I have been arguing again. I can't even remember what started it this time. Why doesn't he ever listen to my point of view? If something isn't his idea then he won't even consider it.

The tinkling water flowing over the stones at the river's edge reminds me of wind chimes. That's another thing. They annoy him. I love them. Their ringing melodies produce a masterpiece of musical magic. He says I need to take them down. But I won't. I might even go out and buy another one tomorrow. Maybe.

I sit down on a grassy hillock, wrapping my arms around my knees as a flash of blue sweeps past, then another. Two young kingfishers land on an outspread branch a short distance downstream. Their iridescent wings flutter as a parent lands next to them and feeds their gaping mouths.

Ah, to have babies! Jack doesn't want them. I do. Desperately. Although it's probably too late now. I've known since the day he proposed six years ago that he didn't, but kept hoping he would change his mind. He'd had enough of them, being the oldest of eight. He'd helped his mum bring up the two younger ones when his father had become ill. But that was before I knew him. Long before we were married. They are teenagers now so off doing their own things, not babies any longer.

A loud squawking and a beating of wings makes me twist my head. A grey heron comes in to land in the shallow water not three yards from me. Its enormous wings large enough to transport me away to a world where... What sort of world would I prefer? I don't really know.

The bird gives me a beady look. I sit completely still, trying not to blink. Hope it doesn't think I'm a mate, dressed as I am in a grey hoody and shorts. I know I'm tall and have long, gangly legs but surely I don't resemble a heron?

It turns and looks away. I let out my breath in a long sigh as it delves its long beak into the green water and brings out something wriggling and silver. Probably a trout. The sun glints on its shiny scales for a second before it disappears down the heron's gullet. It's a wonder there are any fish left in the river, what with all these birds filching them.

Ah, I remember now. That was what the argument had been about. Should we have fish for dinner? I said it was traditional to eat fish on a Friday but he scorned tradition. "That was in the old days. It doesn't pertain to life now," he had said.

Pertain? Why does he have to use such old-fashioned language? Nobody uses words like that any more. But, of course, I didn't say so. Biting my tongue, I gave in, as usual, and took the pork chops out of the freezer to defrost.

A moorhen swims by, followed by four little fluffy black chicks, all tweeting loudly, trying to gain their mother's attention. She alights on the bank. Her green legs and feet look incongruous against her black body. See, I can use long words when it suits me.

She doesn't look round as she waddles off into the reeds, trusting the chicks to follow. One of them doesn't. It carries on swimming. A free spirit. An independent soul. 'Good for you,' I say. But then it realises it's on its own and, squeaking, it turns, jumps out, and runs after the others. Maybe it's just as well. Safer.

A cool breeze ruffles my long, auburn hair. Maybe I ought to have it cut. Jack says I should. But I love the feel of it swishing round my face. He says curls don't suit me, either. That I should straighten it. Dye it, as well. Heck, what's wrong with the colour God gave me? It might have faded a little. But it's still as thick and lustrous as when I was younger. Anyway, I don't criticise his grey, wispy sideboards. I try not to smile when he combs those long strands of white hair over the top of his head to hide his baldness.

Such a handsome man he was once. When I first met him. Like a film star. His greased black hair brushed back into a quiff. A bit like an aging Elvis. Even though that style went out of fashion years ago. Now he's more like that little fat man off the advert for cigars. You know the one? Where they play the tune 'Air on a G string' or something like that?

It's not that he's let himself go. The decline has just sort of crept up on him. Started when he gave up smoking. At least that's something in his favour. Not that he did it to please me. It was the doctor. Told him if he didn't stop, he would be dead in two years. I sometimes wonder if I should have encouraged him to carry on.

I stand up and watch the clouds scuttering across the sky. Scuttering. I think I might have just made that up. I love making up words. Jack says I'm stupid. How will anyone know what I mean if they haven't heard them before? But you know what scuttering is, don't you, clouds? It's what you're doing. Right across the sky. Scuttering. I'll even make up a poem.

There once was a cloud who went scuttering,
Lost its balance and fell in some guttering.
In foul water it lay
For a night and a day.
Dissolving, whilst coughing and spluttering.

But what's the point? Jack doesn't like poetry, either.

'Is there anything he does like?' I ask myself. Well, not a lot. There's football and...football. That's about it.

It's becoming cold. I should have brought my scarf. Or maybe Jack's football scarf. But I'm not allowed to touch his gear, even to wash it. That's sacred. I don't know what he thinks I'll do with it. Throttle him? Mm...

Better be making tracks. The chops won't cook themselves. Will he want baked potato or mash today? I fancy jackets. As long as I don't put too much butter on them. I really ought to lose some weight. Well, that's what Jack says. But I feel comfortable as I am. I'm not obese, only a few pounds overweight. He can talk, anyway. With his paunch, he wouldn't look out of place in an ante-natal clinic. At least eight months gone.

The moorhens and the kingfishers have disappeared. Oh, and so has the heron. I wonder if it found its mate.

I'm by myself. Do I like that idea? Could I manage alone if anything were to happen to Jack? I mean, I've never spent a night on my own in my whole forty two years. Not once. He hasn't ever gone on holiday without me. I suppose he's not such a bad stick. I, on the other hand, often go away with my friends for weekends. Leave him to look after the dog. Well, it is his pet. I was never allowed to have one. But as soon as his brother offered him a puppy, he took one look at it and was smitten. He loves the little yapping runt more than me. I'm sure of that. But then anybody would. How can I compete with those big brown eyes? My small green orbs with their stumpy eyelashes don't stand a cat in hell's chance. I'm told that all the time.

My stomach rumbles. I should have brought a snack with me, knowing I was going to be out for a while. Well, at least Jack won't go hungry. Not with the delicious ham and mustard sandwiches I left him. I made a special effort with them.

I drag my feet, checking my watch. Have I been out long enough?

I meander back along the lane. A blackbird sings from a tree above me. I stop to listen. My favourite song. I could listen to that sound all day long. Sing on, Blackie.

Maybe we could go bird watching tomorrow. I heard there was a rare sighting of a marsh warbler the other day. Over the hill the other side of the village. I've never seen one. Don't think Jack has, either. I forgot to tell him about it. Better hurry back. Something to look forward to.

I begin to run. I shouldn't have stayed out so long. What was I thinking?

It's beginning to drizzle. I put up my hood and run faster. The rain is now pelting down. I have to dodge the puddles. My trainers squelch as I weave in and out.

There's nobody about as I approach the house. That's unusual. Absolute silence. No music from Jack's infernal radio. Or yapping. I approach the back door. It won't open.

'Jack, are you there?'

What's stopping the blinking door? Why can't I open it?

'Jack?''

I push and push. Something's stuck behind it. It feels like a dead weight. My heart begins to thump. Then I hear a kind of keen wailing. It gets louder. It sounds like Jasper.

No, no, please God, please don't let me be too late. I shouldn't have put that stuff in those sandwiches.

THE CLOCK

My lounge is so full
of my treasures,
I don't know
where I should start.
With ornaments
made by my children,
I know all their
features by heart;
a blue bird, its beak
all awry now,
a white cat that is
standing so tall,
but, by far the most cherished
of them all
is the grandfather clock
on the wall.
It was given me lovingly
last Christmas
by the youngest of
my little brood.
I clapped hands and raved,
so delighted,
and wound it up
so well and good.

The clear chimes each quarter
I heard them;
how lovely they were…
well at first.
By lunchtime my head
was a reeling,
and by teatime
I'd started to curse.
I needed to find
a solution,
but couldn't upset him,
now, could I?
He'd presented it to me
so proudly;
so each time it chimed,
with a sigh,
I gritted my teeth, 'til he'd
gone up to bed,
and straightway, out
the batteries came.
Ten o'clock went
so quietly and calmly,
and eleven
exactly the same;
no bells ringing,

no bonging or clanging;
I even stayed up
until midnight.
But what would he say
the next morning
when he'd notice the clock
wasn't right?
Would I tell him the truth,
or say nothing?
But, thank goodness,
the very next morn,
he said, "What a relief,
that noisy clock's stopped.
I think no more could
I've borne."
Its hands now are stuck
at six thirty,
and the pendulum's
halted its swing;
it just hangs on the wall
hushed and forlorn,
and sometimes I yearn
for its ring.

AUTUMNAL MORN

Tall trees sway tranquilly
in the soft breeze,
their green leaves are now turning brown;
black, raucous rooks that roost
in their midst
are today scarcely making a sound.
Ripe acorns swell
in their knobbly green cups,
almost ready to fall to the ground.
In the soft, hazy light
of an autumnal morn
peace pervades for all those around.
Sweet succulent berries,
hanging juicy and black,
their blossom has now long since gone,
soaring swallows are flying
way high up above,
preparing for their journey home;
cream-coloured corn stalks,
all stubbly and sharp,
now that harvesting has all been done;
nectar-rich flowers
are in such short supply,
for the busy bees buzzing in the comb.

Black beetles scuttling
in the dense undergrowth,
filling up their winter larder;
grey stormy clouds are now
scudding along,
and the westerly wind, it blows harder;
As limp, listless leaves fall,
all swirling around,
unable to cling on any longer,
the crisp coldness of winter
is on its way south;
its harshness growing daily ever stronger.

LAMBS (A Thought for the Day)

I have lamby ornaments all around my house and garden and, every year, in the spring, my husband takes me on 'lambwatch', in search of any real ones. The first sight fills me with excitement. I can't explain why. I don't have quite the same experience when I see new-born calves or piglets, as cute as they may be. When we find a field full of ewes and lambs we stop, if it's possible, and I go and talk to them. More often than not, they look at me for a few seconds, and then resume chewing. I once saw twin lambs having a great time climbing on their mother's back and jumping off, as she lay there, seemingly ignoring them. Maybe it's to do with my Catholic upbringing. Jesus is the Good Shepherd, and we are his sheep. He said, 'Feed my lambs, feed my sheep.' Not calves or piglets. I don't eat lamb, by the way. I just can't bring myself to do so, when I think of those little ones frolicking and gambolling in the fields, even though the farmer's wife at the farm shop says she considers them to be troublesome teenagers by the time they go to market.

TOOTH BE OR NOT TOOTH BE

I put in my dentures
one morning at eight,
thinking nothing amiss,
my hot porridge I ate.
Then I swept up the crumbs
to make the kitchen floor neat,
and put them outside
for the songbirds to eat.
But something did tell me
my mouth felt all wrong,
a hole I could feel
when I stuck in my tongue.
When I looked in the mirror,
alas and alack,
there gaping and glaring,
a big gap stared back.
So up to the bathroom
I hurried, forsooth,
for where had it gone,
that elusive white tooth?
I looked in the beaker,
couldn't find it in there.
I searched on the surfaces,
they were all bare.

I picked up the mat
and I looked all around,
but nowhere in there
was my tooth to be found.
I was sure I had had it
the day before, at bedtime,
But it had gone missing,
that teggy of mine.
And then I remembered,
the previous night,
my denture, I'd dropped,
in the dim, fading light,
right onto the tiles
of the hard kitchen floor.
I'd picked it up quickly
and pulled shut the door;
tooth detached from its mooring
never entering my head,
I'd put denture in water,
and gone off to bed.
Now, later next day,
well, in fact 'twas quite dark,
I recalled what I'd done, and so,
just for a lark,
I went with a torch

to the frosty, cold lawn,
to search through the crumbs
I had put out that morn.
Hooray, there, I found it;
what a joy to behold.
I ran back in the house,
so my tooth I could scald,
lest something had fouled it
with rubbish or muck.
Well, I didn't want anything
spoiling my luck.
Then, next morning, to clean them,
the tap I turned on,
but, when I felt in the glass,
that damned tooth, it had gone.
So I set to and searched
round that bathroom again,
but no toothie-peg showed itself.
Oh, what a pain!
I couldn't believe
it had vanished once more.
Now, where could it be?
I let out a loud roar,
and trundled downstairs.
But then into my brain,
crept a thought that perhaps

it had gone down the drain?
So out did I traipse,
that foul pipe to inspect,
full of leaves and detritus,
as one might expect.
I poked and I prodded,
but to no avail;
no sign of said tooth could I find.
Did I wail!
Then one more idea
appeared in my mind.
That under the sink
would be a cup of some kind,
to catch things that idiots like me
drop beneath,
Such valuable items
like jewellery and teeth.
Back upstairs I trudged,
though not really with hope,
and unscrewed the cup,
but then, what a dope!
Forgetful, I emptied it
all down the plug,
and flooded the cupboard
and most of the rug.
But what bliss did I feel,

when I took it downstairs,
and emptied the cup,
though it was full of hairs,
for there lying inside it,
what a lovely surprise,
was my dear tooth, my teggie,
my valuable prize.
So, tooth washed once more,
to the dentist I went,
and off to the menders
my denture he sent.
End of story, you think,
but with one last whack,
you never will guess,
on the day it came back,
as soon as I put it
inside of my gob,
the darned tooth broke off.
Oh, I wanted to sob.
But now it has gone one more time
to be mended,
and hopefully my story
it will then have ended.

A LIMERICK

There once was a lady called Cherry
Who went over to France on a ferry,
   Duty free shop on board
   Sold the wine she adored,
And she drank way too much and got merry.

HIGHWAYHORSE

Why have we stopped here? These woods look very dark and sinister. Rather scary, in fact. I don't think I like them. Oo, what was that? Phew, only a magpie. Morning, Mister Magpie, how are your wife and...? Oh, all right, fly off, then, I was only being friendly.

I can hear hoof beats. They're coming towards me. Oh, heck. What if they're dangerous people, like those we had to run away from last night? Oh, thank goodness, my rider's taking me behind some trees. I can stamp my hooves and keep warm. I can't see now, though. I won't know if they are nice or nasty folk. I suppose it's just as well.

They're coming closer. I can hear jingling bells. It sounds like a sledge. Maybe, if I peep through the leaves I might see something. That's better. But they aren't horses; they are some peculiar animal with long pointy horns. That front one looks so funny. He has a red nose. Ha, ha, he must be cold. Oh, and just look at the driver. A big, fat chap, dressed in red, with a long white beard, and the sleigh is full of lots of coloured parcels.

He doesn't look frightening. Quite the opposite. He keeps saying, 'Ho, ho, ho.'

Goody, good, we're moving into the open. I might be able to have a chat with those unhorse animals.

But what's that my rider's saying? Surely not today?

Here we go again.

"Your money or your life."

ME DROP OFF TO SLEEP?

Me drop off to sleep?
Oh, if only I could,
but this incessant din
it on and on goes;
a caterwauling cacophony
of veritable sound
that merely increases
the depths of my woes.

Each night as I think
I'll nod off to sleep,
it starts, in crescendos
loud and shrill,
and once more I find
I am now wide awake.
Oh, why didn't I take
that sleeping pill?

Those dozens of sheep
will not aid me at all,
nor even
ten thousand or more.
I lie here awake,
trying to cover my ears,

feeling rattled
and grieved to the core.

So shrill is the din
that the neighbours must hear.
They surely will be
So very vexed.
Each note is pitched higher
and booms more with each breath.
They'll be wondering
what melody is next.

I should make a tape
of the decibel level,
for I know that
he never believes me.
He says I embellish
and exaggerate,
and that *I* drone
like a demented bee.

I even went out
and bought him a ring
to wear on his
left, little pinky;
his finger, of course,

you must understand,
not his other – um
little pinky winky.

I lie there awake.
Where have I gone wrong?
But maybe
I'm speaking too soon.
For what's that I hear?
Is it silence at last?
Ah, thank goodness,
it's a soundless tune.

NIGHTMARE

The cottage looked just like the gingerbread cottage in the Hansel and Gretel story. A bluetit flew out of the roses growing up the stone walls as Marcie turned the key in the lock and cautiously pushed open the old, oak front door. It creaked a little but she found the sound reassuring. She couldn't explain why. Perhaps it reminded her of her grandmother's house outside Bridlington where she had often stayed in the school holidays, and had spent so many happy times.

She put down her bags in the hall and peeped into the front room. An old shabby, probably red, settee and an armchair that had also seen better days filled its tiny space. No television, she noticed, but then she had come for peace and quiet, so what would she want with one?

A strange, fusty smell pervaded the room, so she tiptoed inside and opened the little leaded window. A robin, singing to its mate outside, would be all she needed for company.

Deciding a cup of tea would be welcome, she went through to the back kitchen. Old pipes rattled as she turned on the tap to fill the kettle, and the water looked rather brownish, so she let it flow until it ran clear. Matches, to light the stove. A rummage in her handbag produced a box. Thank goodness she had remembered them.

A soft sound from above made her look up. Nothing there, except a few cobwebs in the corner of the ceiling. It had probably been the wind blowing in the eaves.

She drank her tea and took her suitcase upstairs to unpack. Grateful that someone had left moth balls in the single wardrobe, she hung up her clothes. The camphor offset the mustiness. Would her sheets be damp? She didn't know how long it had been since anyone had stayed there. She drew back the flowery quilt and gave it a shake. Maybe there would be a hot water bottle somewhere. That would freshen it. She found one in the airing cupboard and, while her soup heated through, she filled it, making sure it had not perished, and took it up. Had the stairs creaked when she had gone up before? She hadn't noticed it, but they definitely did that time.

After her tea she took her favourite Jane Austen novel, Pride and Prejudice, up to bed and read for an hour, deciding that an early night would be in order, because she wanted to be up bright and early the following morning,

As she dropped off to sleep, an eerie sound pervaded her semi-consciousness, reminding her of events long forgotten, things she did not want to remember. She tossed and turned, sweat running between her breasts.

See page 67 for part 2

BLUETIT'S REVENGE

Oh, look, there's a bluetit.
It's trying in vain,
to get into my kitchen,
come in out of the rain.
So cheekily perched
on the white window ledge,
tip-tapping. Be careful,
you'll fall off the edge.
Tip-tappety, tappety,
let me come through,
I can see you inside
and I want to join you.
There's nothing to stop me,
as far as I know,
so why can't I get through
this blinking window?
He's pecking away
at the clear window pane,
and peeping inside.
There he goes again.
What on earth can he want
in this old house of mine?
I've no juicy caterpillars
on which he might dine.

I'll flip-flap my wings,
try a different pose,
and I might then get in
through that stupid window.
I'm sure they will like me,
without any doubt,
but if I can't enter,
they'll never find out.
I'll go fetch my camera,
this sight I must catch,
of a bluetit sat cheeping
on my closed window latch.
Or shall I just open it
and see his intent?
But if I approach,
will he fly off, hell bent?
Well, I don't understand
why I cannot get through.
The glass looks all clear to me.
I might as well poo
all down the darned window,
prove I mean business.
Ah, now I feel better.
Hope they appreciate the mess.

SPARROWS (A Thought for the Day)

I hate discrimination of any kind and like to think I am not racist, but watching the birds in my garden, I wonder if I am to a degree. You see, the sparrows—plain brown little birds, until you look closely and see the intricate patterns of their feathers—seem to take over. There are so many more of them than any other bird. I want to say, 'Go away, you plain little bird, and let the pretty ones come in, like the goldfinches, with the yellow streaks on their wings, and their red heads; or the robins with their red breasts.' But when I actually study the sparrows, they amuse me. What one does, the others copy; and they hop about the garden, chirping away, much to my husband's chagrin. The goldfinches, on the other hand, come and take their fill of the niger seeds, and the seeds in my dead cornflowers, and then fly away, without a by-your-leave.

There is a place for all God's creatures on our earth, and we must appreciate each and every one's diversity. We can't all be the same.

THE PRESENTATION

"I present the nominee for this new award…"

Shaking with excitement, George eagerly awaited the names.

"The nominee is George Brown."

Only his name had been put forward. Fancy that! His first year at the firm, and he had to be the winner.

Of course, it was only to be expected. He was already the most popular member of staff ever to have worked there. He had reorganised the files; retimed the rotas—he preferred a late lunch break—and rearranged the seating plan. Well, no-one else would be bothered about having a seat near the window to watch the swans down on the lake, would they?

Everyone said what a transformation he had made. Even the managing director had called him into his office and, although he hadn't said so in as many words, he had more or less told him he would win.

How proud Philomena must be. His mousy little wife had never won anything in her life.

Preparing to stand, his acceptance letter at the ready, he watched the MC open the envelope.

"It gives me great pleasure to present this new award for..." The MC looked around the room, maintaining the suspense. "For the most supercilious, rambunctious, arrogant and pompous employee this firm has ever had the misfortune to grace its staffroom."

Ignoring the raucous applause, George tipped up his chair, grabbed Philomena's hand, and legged it out of that hall faster than a rat out of a drainpipe.

FREE-FALLING
Written as my oldest sister was dying

For how much longer am I here,
my eyes no longer seeing?
The black abyss is what I fear;
Falling, falling, falling.

The sounds I hear are far too low.
Please, just a moment more.
I really do not want to go;
Stalling, stalling, stalling.

Bright lights I see way up above,
Are they the hopes and prayers
Of all the people that I love,
Calling, calling, calling?

One final breath and then I'll leave.
All right, I'm coming now,
To meet my maker, I believe.
Free…fall…ing.

NOT WORKING

Today I won't be working hard,
I can't be bothered to.
My legs are aching, full of pain,
no matter what I do.
Those people sitting there are laughing;
someone tell me why;
I'm only going through my act.
If only I could fly!
For then I wouldn't have to walk
on legs that hurt me so,
I'd beat my wings and rise up high
or flutter way down low.
I'd soar to heights unknown before
and see things never seen
by beast or animal on earth,
go places I've not been.
Oh, wouldn't that be wonderful?
To leave this drudge and toil,
and wander round the world outside
and tread on different soil.
But no, it wouldn't happen so,
I'll never leave this place.
I'm doomed to stay my whole life long,
remain in this rat race.

All right, all right, I'll stand right up
and wave my feet about,
but don't expect a startling show,
I'm sure my toe's got gout.
For a circus elephant just like me
does really have no choice
but do all that he's told to do,
and obey his master's voice.

COINCIDENCES *(A Thought for the Day)*

Some people believe there are no such things as coincidences—that everything happens for a reason. I am one of seven sisters and, a year or so ago I went to my youngest sister's in Littlehampton for her surprise sixtieth birthday party. We had a lovely weekend until another sister and I were coming home on the Monday morning. We had inadvertently booked different trains, but we persuaded the guard to let her catch my train, as the weather had turned bad and trains were being delayed. After about half an hour we stopped, soon being informed that there'd been a fatality on the line ahead and no trains could get through to London. We didn't notice the wait as, after saying a silent prayer for the deceased person, we sat chatting, and time flew. Eventually, we were taken back to Haywards Heath and a bus was put on to Gatwick and we were able to continue our journey northwards. I finally arrived at Nottingham two and a half hours late. Now, if I had been on my own, I would have declared it to be a nightmare journey, but as I had my sister's company, it took away most of the angst.

Was it a coincidence that the weather had taken a turn for the worse, so we could travel together, or divine intervention?

ODE TO MY MOTHER

In lonely childhood you were left
all on your own, no one to love,
'til we arrived to help you sew
life's tapestry, that so well you wove.

You suffered much throughout your life,
but bore it all with patient calm.
Your faith was as a beacon bright,
enriching us with soothing balm.

When we were young you moulded us,
taught us to know the wrong from right;
filled us with love; we felt cocooned,
throughout every day and night.

You were the mainstay of our lives,
arms open wide, with loving smile.
We looked to you to steer and guide.
You understood each whim and wile.

SIX GEESE A-LAYING

"Come on, girls," Gillian called to her six white geese, waddling along on the other side of the lake. One by one they jumped into the murky, brown water and swam across to her.

She had bought the birds a few months earlier, intending to set up a market stall, selling eggs, along with vegetables from her kitchen garden. Sadly, they had not lived up to their promise and had not laid a single one.

She shooed her 'girls' into their night shelter, slamming the bolt across the door. Perhaps, that night would be different, and they would provide her with a nice surprise the next morning. After all, what better present could she have for Christmas?

During the night, loud cackling woke Gillian. Were her geese being attacked? She jumped out of bed and ran to the window. The moonlight lit up the silhouette of a fox, sloping away into the woods.

Should she go down and check on the girls?

Shivering, she peered out towards their hut. She could just make it out. It didn't look damaged. All had gone quiet once more, so she climbed back into bed.

"Happy Christmas, Mum." Twelve-year old Rory was tapping her shoulder. "Guess what?"

Gillian opened her eyes. Rory beamed as he held out a dish. She looked inside it. Six large, white eggs. Her geese had finally laid.

Thank you, Mister Fox, for giving them such a scare, she thought.

COMPETITION PAGE

Each day I scan the papers for
the competition page.
If answers somehow I can't get,
then I am filled with rage.

The crosswords are my favourites,
but not the cryptic ones.
I can't tell what on earth they mean,
especially the puns.

My poor dog hates it when I moan
and scratch my perplexed head.
He cries and whines until I stop,
to take him out, instead.

But all the while I'm walking him
my mind is in a whirl.
If only I could get the ten across,
my fists I could unfurl.

I hurry home and grab the pen,
the seven down I've found.
I've finished it, oh joy of joys,
I jump and dance around.

But, no, I've not. I'm sorely vexed,
for when I look again,
the sixteen down's eluded me.
I have to blame my pen.

It must have run out when I wrote
the answer to that one.
For sure I can't have missed it,
so, wherever has it gone?

INTERLOPERS (A Thought for the Day)

Whilst on holiday in the Lake District I love to watch the many different types of birds. However, interlopers come and eat most of the peanuts that I put out—grey squirrels. Now, if they were red squirrels, I would be overjoyed, as I have never seen one, even though the blurb for the log cabin says they should be abundant in that area. Maybe that was written before the greys took over. But the greys are part of the scenery, now. They are here to stay. It makes me wonder if I am being racist, or animalist, if that's a word. Is that how I view foreigners coming into my country? Do I consider them to be interlopers? I try not to. As far as I can see, they are only trying to make a living and feed their families, just as we are. Their colour might be different in some cases, but in God's eyes there is no difference. We all belong to one human race. I believe we need to view each other as brothers and sisters, not with resentment or ill will, but appreciate the various talents and abilities we can each bring to enrich our world.

MOO

I've drunk mugs full of coffee
and cups of tea too,
I've had so much milk
that now I say, 'moo'.

If I am not careful
I'll be chewing the cud,
and rolling round, starkers,
in the dirt and the mud.
My tail will be whisking
to scare off the flies
that get down my ear'oles
and into my eyes.
They'll be calling me Bessie
or Daisy or…Bert?
No, that would be silly.
Now I am no flirt,
But if I drink too much milk,
will an amorous bull
creep up behind me?
Think I'm on the pull?
Will he say 'Not for me,
no artificial insemination,'
and jump on my back

without hesitation?
Now I'm just being fanciful
and ludicrous too.
A bull won't look twice at me,
'cos I can't really moo.

PETER'S NEW BIKE

"But I can't!" Peter wailed for the third time.

"Just try once more," his grandfather tried to encourage him. "I know it's hard, but you mustn't give in."

He knew his granddad was being thoughtful, but he wondered whether he'd ever regain the skill he used to have, like when he'd won the county's under-eleven cycling championship the previous year. But that was before...

"I'll try once more then, Granddad."

He cocked his good leg over the brand-new bicycle, his favourite colour, a cool red, and finding his balance at last, rode off. Down the hill he flew, the wind almost taking his breath away.

"I did it, I did it!" he yelled at the top of his voice when his granddad caught up with him.

"I'm so proud of you," his granddad said huskily. "After your leg was crushed in that accident I wasn't sure if you'd ever walk again, let alone ride a bike. Well done!"

"I thought I'd never ride again, as well. Thanks for buying it, Granddad, it's the best birthday present I could have wished for."

NIGHTMARE Part 2

The smooth, crystal lake shimmered beside Marcie as she set up her easel and paints. Would she be able to capture its beauty? Nothing stirred in the still, early-morning light as she picked up her paintbrush and pointed it towards the canvas. Pictures of animals and birds she had never seen before appeared. She could not stop. That was not what she had wanted to create, that monstrosity of vibrant colours. Her idea had been a soft melody of pale, thoughtful shades, not strident blacks and browns.

The brush moved on and on, as if it had a mind of its own. More and more canvases became covered in the awful melee. Canvas upon canvas, creature upon creature, filling the whole glade in which she stood, helpless to prevent it, until she could no longer see the lake or the trees surrounding it, or even the space between her and the easel. She was becoming enveloped by the monsters, her breath squeezed out of her body.

A scream echoed around the clearing, horrible in its intensity. What or who could have produced it?

Marcie opened her eyes, realising it had come from her own mouth. She could not feel her heart beating, or her chest moving. Her hands were as cold as ice. Had she died?

See page 100 for the final instalment.

FADING EYESIGHT

The book told a tale
about a byegone age;
I could hardly wait
to turn each page.
I read and I read
'til the light grew so dim,
but just one more chapter
I wanted to skim.
So, why, tell me why
had the words all gone small?
My eyes must be ruined,
I'd best make a call
to the opticians in the morn
to save my fading eyesight
and buy some new specs,
then I can read all night.

BIRDSONG (A Thought for the Day)

I woke up the other morning to the sound of unusual birdsong outside my bedroom window. As dawn had not quite broken, I saw no point in jumping out of bed to find the binoculars to see what kind of bird was greeting me so loudly. I lay there, listening to the beautiful sound, saying prayers for all God's bountiful goodness. The bird sang on and on, as if willing me to get up. After a while, I did so, but couldn't see any sign of it. Was it in the tree at the bottom of the garden? Or did it have such a projective voice that it sang from the bottom of the allotments nearby? Whatever, the answer, I couldn't see it. It made me wonder if God's voice is like that. We hear it from a distance, but never see him. Do we listen to it, or do we pull the duvet over our ears and try to blot it out? Do we seek out the binoculars and try to find him, or shake our heads and put the kettle on, thinking, 'if he doesn't show himself, why should we make an effort to find him'?

ROSES

It had always been Freda's dream to end her days in the countryside, in a cottage with roses growing around the door, and now her suitcases were packed and ready. The cottage in the brochure looked just what she had dreamt of, so when Horace had suggested they move in together, she had readily agreed. She closed her eyes and leant back, dreaming of the two of them toasting crumpets on a toasting fork in front of the fire, or holding hands and staring lovingly into each other's eyes.

Horace had magnanimously told her he didn't expect her to darn his socks, just do a bit of cleaning and cooking. Not much, mind, along with his washing—including his dirty underpants, she supposed.

A glance at the clock told her that her daughter would be arriving in about ten minutes. Could she get away before Molly arrived? Molly did not approve. She did not like Horace, and when she had shown her the picture of the quaint little cottage, she had scoffed at it. But, surely she would not deny her dear old mum some happiness?

Picking up her suitcase, she hesitated. Then she spat on the brochure, ripped it up and threw it in the bin.

'Damn you, Horace Winterbottom. Molly's just won the lottery. I'd rather go and live in her new mansion. It may not have roses around the door, but it sure beats being your skivvy.'

MEMOIRS
Chapter 2: Pets

Myself, when young, did yearn for a pet of my own. When I was three or four we had a family cat called Raffy, who I remember as being grey and long-haired. Mostly feral, though, he would stay out for days at a time, living off mice and rats on the farm. So he wasn't really a pet, and certainly not mine.

"We can't afford a pet. I struggle to feed the six of you," my harassed mother would reply to any plea from me.

My father kept chickens and I would toddle along beside him at feeding time, carrying their bowl of food—potato peelings mixed with some sort of meal. Then, one day, the cockerel chased me, giving me nightmares for weeks. Chickens were definitely not pets!

Dogs were an animal I would never dream of having. I was terrified of them. No idea why. I don't remember ever having had a bad experience with one. My mother, who didn't usually pander to any of our foibles, used to have to plan walks to the village along routes where she knew there wouldn't be any dogs barking at gates that we might pass.

My mother finally relented to my pleas when a neighbour's cat had kittens and I and one of my sisters were allowed to choose one each before the rest were drowned—the usual method of disposal in those days if a home couldn't be found for them straightaway. However, it only lived for a few months. My youngest sister cuddled it so hard that its innards started to fall out and it had to be put down. I was devastated and cried for days. The other kitten didn't fare much better. It was run over by a tractor.

As we lived on a farm we were allowed to play out of doors and roam free for hours at a time. I used to collect birds' eggs, a practice that is now illegal. Perhaps it was then, but I didn't see the wrong in it at the time. I only ever took one egg from a nest. I knew them all by sight. Robin's were brown with white speckles; blackbird's larger and blue. I used to 'blow' the yolk out, and kept them wrapped in cotton wool in a little box. That box was one of my treasures that I used to take backwards and forwards to boarding school each term to remind me of home. We had a pet budgie for a while, but he was my mother's, not mine.

Then one day when I was about eight my big chance came. One of the boys who lived a few doors away had been given a black Labrador puppy for his birthday. Well, this puppy had cornered a frog in the back garden. Could this be the answer to my prayers? A pet frog wouldn't cost my mum anything, so she couldn't possibly have any objection. I waded through the crowd of excited children who had gathered to watch, scooped up the terrified creature and ran home before anybody could stop me.

I thought back to my previous attempt at taming wild animals. Well, you couldn't call it an animal, or even very wild, it was just a large black beetle that appeared in the front garden, looking lost and lonely. I spent all morning making a house for it out of broken bricks and large stones. The house even had three rooms with little doorways for the beetle to move through. A veritable beetle palace. Then my mother called me in for dinner. I gobbled it down quickly, eager to get back to my new friend. How disappointed I was when I went back outside. No sign of my beetle anywhere. I searched the whole garden but to no avail. Nobody had warned me that beetles could fly so I hadn't thought to add a roof!

Another wild animal that my younger sister and I had planned to tame was a baby rabbit that we found trapped in a wire fence. It was so soft and cuddly. We ran home in excited anticipation, eager to find something to use as a hutch. We settled it into an old cardboard box with some straw and went happily to bed. Unfortunately, when we rushed down to check on it next morning we found one dead little bunny. Daddy told us he thought it had mixamytosis, so it wouldn't have survived anyway.

Before I went to boarding school three of my sisters and I spent a year at an orphanage in Berkshire because my mother was very ill. At Christmas some airmen from a nearby American airbase gave us a party and we were each given a present. Mine was a beautiful doll with long, blonde hair. She remained my constant companion until I was about fourteen. Once we had returned home I would take her out and about the farm in an old pram. I would lift her up and show her all the different animals, explaining what each one was called. One day my mother warned me not to go into the north field as a large new bull had been put there. I was curious to see what the fuss was all about. Why shouldn't I go in there? I had been brought up around cows. They weren't scary. In fact they were almost pets. Why should a bull be any different? It was only a male cow.

I casually picked up my doll and, trying not to make it obvious where I was going, did exactly what my mother had told me not to do.

The bull stood calmly eating grass over the other side of the field, so I climbed over the gate and ventured towards it. It looked up and started to move menacingly towards me. My bravado vanished. I turned and ran, vaulting over the gate in one movement, dropping my beloved doll in the process. Fortunately she wasn't damaged, just a little dirty. I never disobeyed my mother again, or thought of bulls as friendly male cows.

Anyway going back to the frog, I found a rusty old Oxo tin in the garden. That would do for his bed. I picked some large leaves from Daddy's cabbage patch, making sure I only chose the yellowing ones we wouldn't be eating, and arranged them in the tin for its blankets. It looked so snug in there. Thrilled to have my own pet at last, I was on top of the moon. However my euphoria was short-lived, as usual. Two days later my mother couldn't stand the smell any longer, even though it was kept outside in the back garden. I was made to dispose of my precious pet. Even though I had fed it muddy water—I had discovered that it opened its mouth if I squeezed the sides—it hadn't brought it back to life. You see, it had been dead all along, but I had been so desperate I hadn't cared.

NATURE

Wonderful willows
waving flexible fingers;
ravens raucously roosting;
swallows soaring skyward,
fleetingly flying,
bumblebees busily buzzing;
sweet, succulent strawberries
rapidly ripening;
badgers bravely burrowing;
sparkling sunshine
showering silvery sunbeams;
Nature's naturally nurturing.

ANGEL VOICES

I'm bored. I feel like I've wandered lonely on this cloud all day. Not a soul has come near, not even a buzzard, or a midge. I've sat here, playing my harp until my fingers are sore, almost cut to the bone, in fact.

Oh, my! Look at that enormous black cloud over there. I don't want that to come anywhere near me. **'Stay away, Stormy. Keep to your own hemisphere.'**

Phew, thank goodness, he's blown away in the opposite direction. I would have been soaked if he had come even close.

Ah, there's a cute little, fluffy cumulus floating towards me.

'Hello!'

Be like that then. Don't speak. See if I care. Just because you don't have an angel on your back.

Oh, no, hold onto your harps, here comes… Wow, that was a strong breeze. Nearly knocked me off. Almost got my wings in a twist.

Better play some more music before my cloud evaporates beneath me. What shall I play? Air on a harp string? Maybe it will entice some of the younger angels to come and listen. Some of them don't have a clue. They play this modern stuff. None of us oldies like it. The Master seems to, though. You can see him tapping his toes when they are practising. Well, you'll never get me playing it. Stick to the old favourites like 'Highway to Hell'. Woops, perhaps not that one. 'Stairway to Heaven' might be more appropriate.

I think I'll call it a day. My cloud has nearly disappeared. Hope I don't get into trouble for not saving any souls.

THE GENTLEMAN ON THE BUS

So where is he going to,
that man sitting there?
He looks so refined
with his slick, silver hair.
But why is he travelling
today on my bus?
Well, he's making no sound,
not creating a fuss.
And why does he wear
such a smart-looking coat?
It looks like it's made
from an angora goat.
Now tell me, who'd sport
such a tiny moustache?
They're no longer in fashion,
but he does cut a dash.
So where is he off to,
this smart gentleman?
Perhaps he's going abroad,
needs to top up his tan.
Oh, what's that he's holding?
It looks like a case
that would hold a guitar
or perhaps double bass.

And is that a trilby
he has in his hand?
Perhaps he once played
in a famous jazz band.
Then why not catch cabs
like the other celebs,
instead of slumming it here
with the rest of us plebs?

LIKE A BIRD

Wee, this is fun. That nest felt so hot and stuffy I couldn't wait to escape. My heart jumped into my mouth, though, when I looked over the side and saw all that empty space outside. But it was worth the wait, just as Mum said it would be.

Oops, I nearly fell then. Perhaps I'd better sit on this branch for a moment and catch my breath. That's better. Now, let's try again.

Ooooooooo, how good does that feel? It's brill. The air tickles your feathers as it rushes by.

I'd better go and tell the others. They were rather apprehensive about coming out, and told me to try it first.

Now which is the way back? Oh, heck, I think I'm lost already. My first venture out and I'm lost. No, wait a minute; that looks like Mum over there.

"Cooee, Mum!"

Why isn't she answering? Perhaps it isn't her. Silly me, that's nothing like her. Our mum has a white spot under her chin, and she doesn't have a red head.

Is that her over there, then? Oh, I'm so confused.

Say, that looks like Bertie flying towards me. Yes it is. "Hi, Bertie!"

"Can't stop, Benjie. I haven't figured out how to land yet."

"Just hover over the branch and lower your wings. Yes, that's right."

"Phew, it's hard work, isn't it, this flying?"

"Yeah, but it's so worth it, once you get the hang of it. Watch me, I'm going to fly right to the top of that tree over there."

"Benjie, come back. Mum said not to go far."

He always was a bit of a weakling, needing Mum's attention more than the rest of us. I'll be fine.

Phew, it's rather high up. Perhaps I better had go back, after all. The breeze nearly blew me over just then, and Mum may be looking for me.

MY FAMILY TREE

What fun I have had,
so much time have I spent,
compiling my family tree.
I've searched right from Scotland
as far down as Kent
for a black sheep;
but none could I see.
I'm quite disappointed.
The nearest I saw
was my grandmother's
auntie's great niece;
or was it her great auntie's
sister in law?
Well, she was married four times,
once to a priest!
Great Grandfather's son,
William's daughter,
got spliced
to a most courageous knight,
but children for them,
in vain have I sought;
his lineage has ended;
no more knights in sight!

Great Auntie Jemima
was wed to George Black,
their offspring
were Freddie and Jane.
When Jane Black wed John Smith,
who was always called Jack,
I guess a blacksmith
was what she became!
I've found out the difference
that I never could name
'tween first cousins
and cousins removed;
If your great grandma
and mine are the same,
second cousins we are,
so I've proved.
It's only if one
generation is missed,
and my aunt is
the one you relate to,
you're a cousin removed.
Just study the list.
It's quite easy
when you know how to.

A DAY IN THE WOODS

Walking through the woods, I stumbled across an old log. Usually, when I'm out walking, I love to sit and survey my surroundings, listening to birds singing their melodious songs, watching colourful butterflies dancing in the breeze. But that day my attention was caught by a very large mushroom, or it might have been a toadstool. I can never tell the difference. I'd heard of big puffballs exploding, and I didn't fancy being showered with spores and becoming a breeding ground for baby mushrooms—or toadstools, whatever they were. They germinate quickly, and I had visions of arriving home, looking like a big pin cushion covered in—not pins—but baby fungi.

I was so tired I had to rest so, eyeing the monstrosity with great trepidation, I sat down on the far side of the log, wiped my sweaty brow, giving the handkerchief a good shake and shoving it back in my pocket before any stray pores could invade it.

Should I open my rucksack and eat my picnic? Well, maybe just the drink. If I put the bottle to my lips quickly, I could have a swig and replace the lid without any of the little blighters climbing in.

Before I could savour said drink, I jumped up. Something had begun to stir. Could it be the mushroom?

No, when I looked down I saw, not spores, but red ants, and they were enjoying a hearty breakfast at my expense. So much for being bothered about toadstools!

EASTER SUNDAY SPECTACLE

The most amazing sight I ever saw
was earlier this morn,
just as the dawn began to break,
as the Easter day was born.
A bright red column as if of fire,
that pillar of colour rose
from the horizon to the clouds;
at the bright pink hue we froze,
and stood and gazed in wonder and awe;
not one of us had seen
a spectacle so stunning or rare;
such a sight had never been.
No doubt remained in anyone's mind,
Our Lord has risen today.
He surely has, it is so clear
upon this Easter day.

THE RING

I look at the ring. It's perfect, just what I want. The blue jewel sparkles at me, inviting me to pick it up. I look around. The shop assistant doesn't appear to be taking any notice of me. She's too busy studying her nails. She must have left the ring out by mistake. Very silly of her!

Will it fit? That's the question. I look at it again. Surely it's even brighter than before. Yes, it looks the right size. I have to have it. I know the jewel isn't real, but I don't care. It's just what I had imagined. The dream ring!

Then I spot the price tag lying beside it. I'd never be able to afford that. Surely a fake wouldn't cost that much? Only one thing for it!

I deftly reach out and touch it. Is she looking? I peep under my eyelashes in her direction. No, still picking at her nails.

My fingers slowly enfold the object of my desire and I gradually withdraw my arm from the counter.

Trying to look nonchalant I begin to edge towards the door.

"You buying that ring or what?" comes a voice from behind.

'E looks a shifty character, to be sure. I'd better keep my eye on him. I'll be subtle though, pretend I 'aven't clocked 'im. I'll just look like I'm absorbed in me nails.

I 'ope Mr Jones, me manager, doesn't come back yet, or I'll get a right rollicking for leaving the ring out. I should 'ave gone over and put it straight back in the cabinet as soon as I realised, but you 'ave to 'ave a bit of fun now and again, don't yer?

I wonder if 'e knows it's a fake. Suppose so. You wouldn't find a genuine sapphire ring in a place like this, especially at that price.

'E's moving. Thinks I can't see 'im. Must think I'm a right bimbo, just because I'm blonde. Well, I'll show 'im.

"You buying that ring or what?"

THE GARDEN

I look out at my garden lawn
and there, what do I see?
A small red-breasted robin,
coyly peering up at me.
His head he then cocks sideways,
bright and shiny is his eye,
His beak he opens, and, oh my!
I think that I will cry
with wonder, for my startled ears
I just cannot believe,
so tuneful and melodious,
each sonorous note does weave
into a symphony of awesome sound,
that thrill me and enthrall,
'til he flies off and joins his mate,
perched cockily on a wall.
Red tulips and blue crocuses
wave prettily below,
their faces open to the sun,
their petals all aglow.
Anemones and primroses,
all vying for a space
with daffodils and narcissi,
their presence they do grace.

The silver birch sways haughtily
above the holly bush,
which shelters twittering sparrows.
All of a sudden, with a whoosh,
a sparrowhawk swoops down
and grabs the nearest one, before
it disappears high above,
its victim in its claw.
The other sparrows squawk and squeal
so loud they put to flight
the white doves roosting in the cote,
who fly up of sight.
I look again for my feathered friend,
but him I cannot see.
Once more my garden is at peace,
so I sit down for my tea.

HOMESICK

How homesick I feel already. I check my watch. Is it really only an hour since I was waving madly to my parents who had come to see me off at the bus stop? My mother looked rather sad as she wiped a tear from her eye.

I watch the purple-headed mountains behind my home disappear as I stare out of the window, and I'm already longing for the end of term. My red hat and gloves, new today, are so warm and snug. We went to buy them—my mother and I—yesterday. We had such a good time, looking round the shops. Then we found a quiet café off the High Street and had afternoon tea. Umm, I can still taste those delicious scones, smothered in jam and cream.

My boarding school looms closer and closer as the bus drives nearer and nearer. But what's that? It looks like… It is. Wow! It's a peacock, strutting down the road beside us. What an unusual sight! Its bright blue feathers gleam in the sunshine. That's cheered me up, and made me smile.

Perhaps boarding school won't be quite so daunting after all.

SCARDEY CAT

"Oh, what on earth was that?"

I scramble under the bed to see if there's anything there. Only a pile of fluff. So what could have caused the peculiar sound I just heard?

There it is again. I quiver with fear. Wouldn't you just believe it? Here am I, having just spent the night all alone and there has to be ghostly goings on. At least, it sounded like a ghost. Not that I know what ghosts sound like, if you know what I mean.

'Calm down,' I tell myself, 'there has to be a logical solution.'

Oh no, there it goes again! I climb back into my warm bed and hide under the sheets, curled up in a ball, too scared to move. My fingers stuck in my ears to block out any repeat sounds, I hardly dare to breath.

A sort of metallic sound filters through my fingers. Do ghosts sound metallic? I shudder with fear.

Maybe, if I open the curtains, I'll be able to see if it's still dark outside. If daylight has dawned, surely a ghost wouldn't dare to appear.

Could that be footsteps? Oh, my goodness, it is. But it sounds as if they're outside. At least that means it isn't a ghost. But what could it be? I'm in my mate's flat on the third floor.

I jump out of bed, stubbing my toe on the cabinet. Yelping, I lunge towards the curtains and yank them open.

The ugliest face I have ever seen pops up at the window.

I scream, falling onto the floor, blubbering like a baby.

A moment later, I hear a kind of scraping sound. Is he that desperate to get in?

Peeping through my fingers, I see a hand, holding a cloth, followed by a squeegey, and burst into hysterical laughter.

Why hadn't John warned me that Tuesday was his window-cleaners day?

THE FORGOTTEN PRESENT

Seems like I've been down here behind the settee for weeks. They must have forgotten me, and it looks like they're taking down the decorations. That red bauble that hung above me was so brilliant, when the sun caught it, that different colours spread right around the ceiling, well, as far as I could see, anyway, through the clear top in my box.

Ouch, that fell on my head! Whatever it is, it's blocking my view. I can only see through a tiny hole now. Perhaps I could knock it off if I shake myself a bit. Shake, rattle and roll… That's better, it's fallen off.

Oo, I can feel a hand stroking me. Don't stop, I like it. Doh, it's only picked up the thing that fell on top of me. Hey, come back! Don't leave me here. I'll go crazy if I don't get out of this dark hole soon.

Ah, I can sense movement. The hand is back. Yes, I'm definitely being picked up.

What's he saying? That when he rolled out the wrapping paper to wrap up Millie's present, it was too short, so he put the present away till he could buy some more paper, but then forgot all about it?

Well, thanks for nothing! Shows how much thought went into purchasing me!

NIGHTMARE Part 3

In the gloom of the early morning light Marcie could make out, on the wall opposite, a picture of a cute mother bear, wrestling with its cubs. Surely, if she could see that, she must be alive.

All of a sudden, the bear leapt off the wall and turned towards her, its eyes gleaming like fairy lights on a Christmas tree. How sweet! But before she could stop it, its claws outstretched and menacing, it leapt on her and gauged out her eyes. She could feel blood running down her face as she desperately tried to push the animal away, but then it bit off her hands and the noise it made as it chomped the bones sounded like thunder in her ears.

Eventually, the animal had eaten all of her body, except her head. Even her nose and chin had gone. All that remained was her brain, floating around. The bear could not seem to catch it, though. She could sense its arms floundering about, but somehow, her brain managed to elude the creature.

Its efforts became more and more feeble and, although she could not see it, she knew it was giving up. With one last deafening roar, it vanished.

The discordant ringing of her alarm clock woke Marcie. She reached out and turned it off, her hand shaking, and her breath coming in short bursts.

Not daring to open her eyes at first, she ran her hands down her body. All there.

As she pushed back the quilt and moved her legs, she looked up at a picture on the wall. A cute mother bear, wrestling with her cubs, seemed to be winking at her.

FINAL THOUGHT

Do you ever wonder where people are going, when you see them zooming past on the motorway, often well above the speed limit, or at other times when you're stuck in a traffic jam and nobody is moving at all? I do. I wonder if the speeding motorist might be late for an appointment, or has received bad news and is haring off to a loved one's deathbed. Are the other drivers in the same boat, as they sit patiently in the non-moving queue, or in some circumstances, not so patiently, hooting their horns and drumming their fingers on the steering wheels? I hope not, for they will, more than likely, not make it in time. Everybody seems to be in such a rush to be somewhere else. There's no point only allowing the correct amount of time it usually takes when planning a journey, as it invariably takes longer then expected. Our roads are so congested, with many drivers unwilling to give way, that travelling is no longer a pleasure. At least for the driver. I much prefer to go by bus nowadays, or, for long journeys, by train. What was the slogan the rail companies used to use? 'Let the train take the strain'. That's very apt.

I wish everybody a safe and, if not speedy, journey today, wherever you may be going, whether it's to the shops, on the school run, or farther afield.

Made in the USA
Charleston, SC
06 February 2015